Be the smartest |

STUPIDLY DEEP THINKING

Paul Casselle

Helpful thoughts for an imperfect world

Stupidly Deep Thinking

Thirty mini-essays that make you think…

(Essays were first published between February 2017 - May 2020)

by
Paul Casselle

Written & compiled with Scrivener

First published on 6th July 2020

(Version 101.5P – Print Edition)

ISBN: 9798664150117

The Bit in the Middle Publishing

Contents

"Let's be careful out there."
(Hill Street Blues - 1981-1987 - NBC television series)

Foreword

Many of my readers have urged me to create a compilation of the years of newsletters that have sparked so many heated debates. *Stupidly Deep Thinking* is the result of tens of hours of reading, selecting and editing piles of these often incendiary musings. I guarantee that you will not be able to read these mini-essays without wanting to cheer, swear or punch me on the nose!

I have taken great care in selecting the thirty best pieces from four years of monthly newsletters. So, if you want to be a person who starts interesting conversations, this book will give you a few years worth of wonderfully contentious issues with which to challenge your friends and family.

Paul Casselle
Spain July 2020

Are you a Human Being?
Febuary 2017

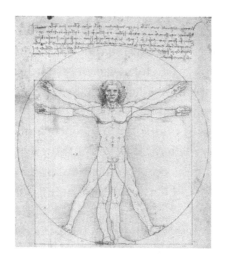

What do I mean by *Human Being*? Well obviously, *Human* refers to our species and *Being* means a living creature. So far, so good. If you are reading this, you are probably a *Homo Sapiens* and most probably a 'critter' and alive.

It is difficult to pin down the first use of the term *Human Being*, but it seems to have appeared for the first time in the 14th or 15th century to describe us. But this is not really what I'm getting at when I ask the question, "Are you a Human Being?" What I want to look at is the noun, *Being*.

Of course, it *is* a noun and is categorised by the

adjective, *Human*. However, what if we read the word, *Being* as a verb? Or to put it another way (you may remember this from your school days) "a **doing** word". So that's my point, are we really *Human Beings* or *Human Doings?*

The standard definition of *Being* is; the fact of existing; existence (as opposed to nonexistence), whereas *Doing* is; the act of performing or executing.

I suppose it's about the difference between physics and philosophy. The former is only concerned with the material; if it can be measured, it exists and therefore is part of our physical universe. If it cannot be measured, it does not exist and is not the concern of the physical sciences. So, where do we put thought, love and ambition? These are not measurable in any physical sense, are they? That is the domain of philosophy and the spiritual.

I remember reading a guide to meditation which explained that most of the time that people spend meditating does not actually achieve their goal. Meditation is when we go into a state of simply existing and definitely not doing. When meditating, if we hear a dog bark, we acknowledge the sound, but must not think about if it's next-door's Labrador and whether he is excited, frightened or about to savage the postman. We must let the sound flow over us without interpretation or reaction. Meditation is the act of being and not doing, and we all find this almost impossible to *do* for any amount of time. Maybe you appreciate the irony of my using the verb 'Do' to describe the act of meditating; 'Being'.

That is not the way living creatures are. We do not simply experience the world; we react and interact with it. We often try to attain some sort of peace, a state of spiritual being, but it is our nature to find practical ways to be alive. So, we are driven to *Do* rather than simply *Be*. Yet, aren't we attempting to achieve a state that we usually reserve for celestial entities and are therefore constantly frustrated by our need to achieve *Being* by *Doing*?

Maybe we need to realise our true nature. Maybe we need to embrace who we really are. We all have a spiritual aspect to ourselves, but our universe-given mode on this planet is not to become spiritual beings in a physical universe, but to accept that our mode of living is mostly one of being practical, at which we are extraordinarily good.

Maybe we need to redefine ourselves as *Human Doings* rather than *Human Beings*.

Should we value the written word?
April 2017

I'll be right up front; yes, I'm biased! Of course I am, I'm a writer.

But are books important to me *because* I'm a writer or am I a writer *because* books are important to me?

I have been interested in the written word since I was very young, but unlike many youngsters, I was less interested in picking up a book that someone else had so kindly already written for me than getting all my own crazy thoughts out on paper.

At the time I didn't know why I was so driven to write rather than choose the less troublesome act of kicking back with a good book, but now, half a century later, I think I know. I wanted to make up my own stories. I wanted to experience life and think, 'what if?'. I wanted to take unrelated events and situations and lock them in a room together, then see what happened.

As I entered the maelstrom years of the teenager and started to rebel against everything I had ever been taught, experienced or thought, I found myself in a white-hot furnace of creative potential, and was drawn to read what others had written. I stumbled onto book after book penned by other confused and troubled people. I realised that I was not alone. I was not going mad. What was happening to me was that I was experiencing one of the greatest gifts the universe has given us; conscious curiosity.

And *that* is what motivated me to write and then to read what others had to say. I have come to realise that I am the sort of person who needs to experiment with the ingredients of cocktails as much as drink them. I am not prepared to consume life passively; this world of ours is an interactive game! And books are one of the best ways we have of connecting with other players.

The non-human creatures on our planet have to suffer the inflexible confines of 'now'. For them life is a conveyor belt of experiences that they react to sequentially. Life simply 'is'. They have no real concept of 'future', and as such are corks bobbing on life's ocean. They have no rudder to direct themselves, and are simply passengers at the whim of the tide. But we have imagination, high-functioning curiosity and the ability to ask 'what if?'. We can imagine hypothetical scenarios of things that have not happened. We can play in a 'yet-to-happen future' that is inaccessible to most, if not all, other living things.

And so that's why I write. I am still that confused young boy that is desperately attempting to make sense of the buzzing in his head. But now I know that that buzzing is a melting pot and a cognitive playground. It is the safe-place where the world delivers events that I can bend, cut, paste and rearrange to my creative heart's content to make sense of the seeming madness. But now that boy has grown up and discovered a world full of others imaginings presented for enlightening consumption by theatre, music and literature.

So, yes, yes, yes, books *are* important. They are endlessly entertaining, incomparable in their scope and value, and thanks to businesses like Amazon, stupidly affordable!

I am in no doubt why I read and write. I write to share my experience of life, and I read to know I'm not alone.

Putting your life on snooze!
May 2017

Every weekday my alarm went off at six AM. I would half open my eyes, hit the button on the watch that was frantically buzzing on my wrist, then turn over and close my eyes again. For a lot of my life the button I angrily hit each morning was marked 'snooze', and this action would magically create, out of thin air, nine extra minutes for me to lie back and thank life for being so kind for adding those additional minutes to the 1,440 that a single day *usually* contained. But I don't need to tell you that that never happened. Those extra nine minutes that I laid in bed were not added to the day, but subtracted from it. Each time I hit that button I went a further nine minutes into debt. And without exception, I would pay the price of that indulgence.

For the last few years, I've started to hit 'stop' rather than 'snooze' when that unwelcome buzzing starts, and then (here's the important bit) even though I may momentarily resist my alarm's clarion call, I get up. But many of us still succumb to the lure of the 'snooze' button even though it often gets us into trouble. So why did I do it for so long? And why do so many of us still do it?

The decisions we make in our everyday lives are influenced by many factors; the options available, what we believe the outcomes will be, and not least, what we would choose if we lived in a universe of one. But we do not live our lives in isolation, so the choices we make do not only have tangible and significant effects on us, but others as well.

The range of options available to us is further confused by what is physically possible (the universe has its own unbreakable Laws), and also what we as individuals are practically and emotionally capable of. This has already become a convoluted labyrinth of social and moral issues, and I haven't even got to the point I want to talk about yet; the human Will.

Once we have picked our way through all the voices in our heads and finally made a decision we believe we can live with, we now need to move on to the most difficult stage; actually doing something, and in this particular case, getting out of bed.

So what is it that gets in the way? Didn't we choose of our own volition to set the alarm at that particular time? What changed between the decision we made last night and our desire to rearrange space and time the next morning? Is it simply hedonism? Are we really that pathetic that we would rather watch Rome burn than get out of a warm bed? I think it is more likely that we have a cognitive separation from the 'future'. What *will* happen is always a fabulous cloud of possibilities until time catches up and forces it to become written onto the indelible pages of the past. We live our whole lives on this extraordinary sliver of time. In some ways the present doesn't actually exist. It is simply the meeting point of the unwritten future and the un-erasable past. And it is at that magical junction where we live our lives.

So maybe our tendency to procrastinate is not hedonism, but hubris, or maybe we are simply allowing ourselves to act naïvely. As we lie in our warm beds we let ourselves believe that the endless possibilities of the future will continue to be a possibility cloud, but as it passes through us and becomes the past, it also becomes a single unchangeable point in history. It is here that we need strength of Will more than at any other time. It is as the future passes through us that we need to be strong and act on our decisions. It is at this point that we need to remember why we decided the night before that we had to get up at that particular time. It is at that point that we need to decide if we want to be caught snoozing at the most important moment of our lives; the precise moment that our future is written into world history.

Knowledge or Peace; it's your choice
July 2017

Is it better to flood our lives with light by striving to know as much as possible or is it sometimes better to retain a few shadows of ignorance in the pursuit of peace?

It has been reported that when Albert Einstein was asked, 'How does it feel to be the smartest man alive?', he responded, 'I don't know, you'll have to ask Nikola Tesla.' I don't know if this quote is true, but I can't help digging deeper. What does 'smart' mean anyway. Is it the accumulation of knowledge, or the speed with which one can recall information, or the freedom with which one can juxtapose such knowledge, or how well one can apply the 'smarts'? And venturing yet another step down the rabbit hole, what's so good about being 'smart' anyway?

It occurs to me that the more I learn, the more I appreciate just how vast is the amount of stuff that is out there to be learnt. Therefore, the more I know, the more aware I become of how proportionally little I actually know. Ironically, the more I learn, the less I know I know! Learning can also be very *more-ish*. The harder I look, the greater the gravity of curiosity sucks me in. And it's a one way trip. Knowledge can be acquired, but not un-learnt. Once you know something you cannot un-know it. And this may lead to getting stuck with truths that with hindsight you would rather have left hidden in the dark. But that is the situation with the benefit of hindsight. Would it really be more comfortable to believe there are monsters afoot, but choose to remain trembling in ignorance? Isn't it the uncertainty of what may be crouching in the shadows that is the primary cause of that most debilitating emotion; fear? Might it therefore be true that our motivation to explore our world is not a hunger for truth, but a desire to allay our fears. Might the most studious of us actually be the most fearful? Is fear the real motivator of learning rather than curiosity?

I *fear* this may well be the case with me. I am scared that I will mess-up and get things wrong if I do not possess all available information; that each piece of the jigsaw I acquire affords me more surety that I am making the best decisions. But I do this at what cost? It is true that the surer I am about something the less mystery persists therefore diminishing fear. That by learning as much as I can, I reduce the possibility of being surprised by things that may *hurt* me, but I also decrease the chance of being surprised by things that may well *enthral* me. My obsessive quest for knowledge may not only risk finding things out that on reflection I would rather not have known, but also dampen down the joy of life taking me by surprise.

My father was a simple man that never wanted to dig too deeply into anything. He would never seek out more knowledge than he needed to get simply from A to B. I have no doubt that he had the intelligence to understand more than he tried to, but he seemed to trade understanding for simplicity, and in so doing lived an uncluttered and rather peaceful existence.

So, might this be the source of my lack of peace? Is it a fear driven desire to know everything that can be known, that leads to an over-taxed mind and a situation where I know more than is good for me? In my rush to gain knowledge and feel safe am I unwittingly trading peace for security, and in so doing causing my own unhappiness? Is happiness simply an act of will; a refusal to live too complicated a life and dig down beyond what is necessary? Or is it a state of delusion? A burying of ones head in the sand and refusing to carry-out a risk assessment as one cannot face the real possibility of 'darkness' existing in the world. Is true courage living side by side with uncertainty or is it the unerring pursuit of dispelling it? Does fear drive us to discover more than we need to, and in so doing destroy the awesome mystery of life that would be the greatest source of the elusive peace we all crave so much?

As usual, the answer seems to be more about balance between two points rather than an absolute black or white choice. Moreover, finding the 'centre of gravity' on this line is probably also different and personal to each individual. Unfortunately, this conundrum seems to belong on that over-burdened shelf marked, 'suck it and see'. Yet again it is down to us as individuals to choose for ourselves where we need to be to find our own equilibrium. Knowledge or peace; the choice is yours.

Cause & effect. Who is in control?
August 2017

Three years ago I moved from England to Spain. I live peacefully with my partner, her two children and our Labradors; forty-five kilometres north-east of Madrid. Last Thursday's terrorist attack in Barcelona challenged me to the core.

The question that keeps drowning out all the other noises in my head is; what do I do? I know I do not hold exclusive rights on feeling guilty about personal inaction; many of us do, but the important thing is that I believe guilt is the way we ennoble our lack of courage, and so perpetuate doing nothing. My problem is not that I know what to do and excuse myself with clever foot-work. Neither am I looking the other way with a solipsistic 'I'm alright, Jack'. I simply feel stuck. I feel too small in the face of this Goliath of evil doing.

I also grapple with a smaller, insidious guilt; that as a member of society, I am culpable, which I believe is true. We are all responsible for each other. But that is not the insidious part of the guilt. The killer thought is that I must be doing something bad to attract such disaster, and I am too weak and need to look to a higher power to forgive and save me. Where could such a self-deprecating belief come from?

The cognitive scientist Steven Pinker often talks of the 'singular *They*'; an overwhelming idea that there is a faceless, but all-powerful group of people who have the real intelligence and clarity, and it is only *They* who can actually do something. But maybe this debilitating creed is simply what *They* want us to believe so *They* can keep control. Are we making this easy for them? Is this notion of *They* simply another way we deflect responsibility like a child to its parents, an employee to their boss or a population to their government.

Just as there is no 'i' in team, I suggest that there is no *They* in a responsible society. This is a major theme in my Bedfellows thriller series; the idea that it is the People (the masses) who have the real power, not the mythical *They*. But the elite are clever and have brainwashed us into believing that *we* are too stupid and simple to even understand the problems, let alone be able to come up with any solutions.

But if I am suggesting that we are not stupid or weak, how do the elite keep this myth alive? They ply us with 'bread and circuses'. Like a drug pusher they convince us that we need them, that we need their protection and hand-outs, that without their stewardship we will fall down and die. It is a lie. The majority have always, and will always, have the power. *They* are nothing without us, but we remain everything whether they exist or not.

To keep us anaesthetised we are kept in a perpetual state of fear. The elite convince young impressionable men that they need to carry-out urban terrorism, and then they turn to us with benevolent arms outstretched declaring that they will protect us. They are offering protection from a danger of their making.

We are society, not *They*. We can make this world anything we want it to be. We do not need them because in reality it is us that actually do everything. It is the People who invent everything. It is the People who produce everything in factories. And it is the People who will decide what kind of society we want.

They are a handful of selfish dictators, we are seven billion passionate, creative and powerful souls. If I ever find myself believing that there is nothing we can do to correct society when it veers towards the cliff edge, I simply need to remind myself how amazing we really are. All we have to do is stop listening to *They*, stop believing the lies they tell us, and believe - really believe the truth - *we* can do this!

Do you know your why?
October 2017

Most of you will know by now that I am no longer en España, but am back in England for my writing course at The Faber Academy (the writing school run by the publisher Faber & Faber).

The classes are only once a week, on Thursdays, but it seemed like a stretch too far to commute every week for six months from Spain. So, here I am in sunny (?) England.

Now, I knew that this was not going to be easy. I am away from my family, I need to find somewhere to live... and I have to create the money to cover it all. But what I didn't expect was to feel nervous. Of course all changes in life are going to come with a little trepidation in tow; a jump into the unknown is by nature a leap of faith, but this is something else. I started to wonder if it was self-doubt.

Recently, I discovered the public speaker, management consultant and author Simon Sinek. He talks about the 'Golden Circle'.

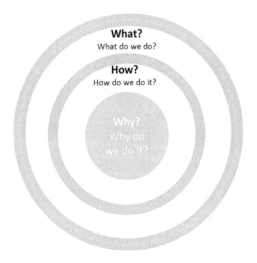

The idea is that there are three concentric circles. Starting from the outside; What, How and Why. Simon Sinek argues that the common human mistake, that holds us back from what we want to achieve, is that we tend to work from the outside in. We all know What we do; we go to jobs, we look after our family and we make decisions to keep us safe and healthy. We also have no problem describing How we do these things, but can you say with clarity Why you do your life?

It's a scary realisation when faced with this simple question that I don't have a convincing answer. And the important thing is not to find a compelling argument to persuade others, but that the very purpose of my life depends on me being able to answer Why to my satisfaction.

At my first class last Thursday, I met the other fourteen writing hopefuls. They are all very interesting people. They are also very bright. Many of them show obvious talent in writing, but what struck me is that as well as being there to learn more about writing, we have all come in search of our Whys; what is the fundamental truth inside each of us.

The fifteen people on my course do not have a problem with what writing is or how one gets words onto a page, my problem, their problem and the cause of much personal disquiet in society is being unclear as to our personal Whys. And moreover, might this be the key to personal success?

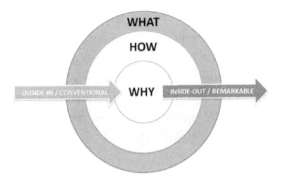

I know what a novel is. A quick look at my Amazon page shows I also know how to write one. I think that that nervousness that surprised me is calling me out and asking me Why I want to be a successful writer? I believe I have some interesting things to say, but until I find why I write, I will remain just another writer in a very large crowd. If I can find my Why, and write and speak from that, the success I am looking for may actually be waiting for me. And I think this may well be true for all of us.

I'll be in touch soon as the writing course (and this journey) unfolds.

Stuck in a rut
October 2017

I am sure that if we all think hard we can remember being involved in some venture or project, that after a time, we discovered was not working out as we had hoped? But despite knowing that we should have thrown down the anchor and stopped, we found ourselves continuing to invest time, money and effort in an endeavour that we really should have abandon.

It's not just you. We all do this, and psychologists have a name for this syndrome. It's called a Concorde Fallacy.

The name comes from the fact that in the 1970s, although the British and French governments became well aware that their super-sonic aeroplane was losing them tons of money and would never be economically viable, they ploughed on. Once they were heavily invested, it was all too easy for them to delude themselves that they should carry on, even though it had become obvious that they should not.

So, what drives such crazy failures of logic. Maybe we simply do not want to lose face or possibly we are refusing to admit to ourselves that we made an error of judgement in the first place. Either way, the Concorde Fallacy is responsible for many very bad decisions in governments, international companies and in our own lives.

As you know, I have just embarked on a very challenging venture. I am taking a writing course with the publisher Faber & Faber in London. The classes are once a week on a Thursday. As I live in Spain, I made the decision to travel to England and live there for the six months of the course. This would be very expensive. The course itself costs many thousands of pounds. Add to that renting somewhere to stay, living expenses and travel, and it is easy to see that this is a very large investment. More to the point, as there is no certainty that these six months will give me the career progression that I am hoping for, it is also a big risk.

My plan was to fly to England and stay with friends until I could find somewhere to rent. Then I would find a part-time job to help fund the venture. It all seemed so possible. It was not long before reality grabbed both of my legs in a vicious rugby tackle. Finding somewhere to rent that was not absolutely horrible, finding a job that would only need me for around three days a week, and most importantly, stopping the whole process from stressing me into an early grave was beginning to look impossible. But I battled on, although it was obvious that I had to find some other way to attend this course. I had committed and invested in living and working in the UK for six months, so that's what I had to do. All my energies were going into making the original plan work. I was well and truly in the grip of a Concorde fallacy.

Even when my mum and brother suggested commuting from Spain once a week instead of trying to live in the UK full-time, I defended and blocked; my mind hung on to my self-delusion with creaky logic and fantasy. Finally, my girlfriend's emotional insistence that I re-address the problem, prised me out of 'hope over reality' and into 'reality über alles'.

So, that demon was finally laid to rest. I have now booked seventeen easyJet flights between Madrid and London. That takes me up to Christmas. So far so good. I've also found an inexpensive hotel and am beginning to get into the weekly commuting thing. It's not perfect, but I am glad I managed to pull my head out of a very flawed plan.

I do have one last thought on the subject, though. Although I am very happy to be over my Concorde fallacy, I really wish easyJet flew one of those supersonic wonders. It would make the trip from Madrid to London in about thirty minutes rather than two hours plus.

When did patience stop being a virtue?
November 2017

Last week I finally succumbed to my twenty-first century desire to listen to music on my iPhone magically without a cable. I made the decision to buy myself a pair of Apple AirPods.

What I noticed is that as soon as I made the decision to buy, I did not want to wait. The deliberation may have taken days, weeks or even months, but as soon as the hammer fell I wanted the goods in my hand. I found myself thinking, whatever happened to patience? When did I acquire this need for instant gratification?

I am from a British generation that remembers when there were only two TV channels, and not only was the choice either BBC 1 or ITV, but they did not even broadcast twenty-four hours a day. Both BBC 1 and the commercial channel finished for the evening around midnight. The BBC with patriotic zeal played its viewers out with the National Anthem.

I remember that there was definitely a feeling of disappointment, but the enforced televisual abstinence gave us a period of quiet where we might intellectually nourish ourselves rather than be spoon-fed media fodder. It also meant that we were encouraged to go to bed at a reasonable time instead of channel hopping like addicted zombies because we were scared we might miss something. This fear of being left out, has now been clinically shown to exist. It has been called **FOMO** (Fear Of Missing Out), and as it is so commonly associated with mobile phones, the term has become **PHOMO**.

So which came first, **PHOMO** or non-stop media? I have little doubt that our propensity for **PHOMO** has lurked deep inside our brains for millennia, but did the media explosion happen organically or is there a manipulative plan behind it? Are we being led to an irresistible banquet for nefarious reasons? And maybe our senses have been so dulled by this twenty-four seven buffet that we are no longer concerned as to which came first; the chicken or the egg, but instead just gorge mindlessly on KFC and omelettes.

You may be thinking, here goes that conspiracy nut Casselle, again, twisting everything into some crazy convoluted story, but I would ask you to consider something I once wrote, 'Nothing happens unless someone wants it to happen.' Or the old detective adage when investigating a crime, 'who benefits?'

All great civilisations that came before us have ended in the same way; distracting the population with bread and circuses while the people at the top fill their coffers by debasing the money. The Romans did it by using increasing amounts of copper in the silver coinage until there was virtually no precious metal left in the coins at all. Today's banks and treasuries are doing it by printing massive amounts of money whose value is based on nothing. Each new note printed devalues every note in circulation causing inflation. Is this the twenty-first century version of adding copper?

Is there a connection between inflation and PHOMO? When my mother was a child, inflation was almost non-existent. She told me how people would save-up for months or even years to buy something. Unlike today, the price of the item would be pretty much the same when finally purchased as when the saving-up started. This is what people were used to. There was little credit, so patience remained a virtue. You wanted something, you saved for it, and when you had enough money you bought it. Inflation destroys this method of acquiring goods as by the time you have saved-up, the price has doubled.

So, we now have engineered inflation, easy credit and twenty-four seven sales channels on TV and the internet. As Oscar Wilde comically observed, 'I can resist everything except temptation.' Have we been led to this land of instant gratification, did we choose the destination ourselves or is it simply the logical conclusion for a technological society?

I think we would do well to look inside our own heads and decide if spoiling ourselves by demanding everything we want instantly is a good thing or if it would be better to reinstate that old virtue, patience.

I chose the latter. It wasn't easy. I was in England

for four days, so I knew I would soon be passing through Luton airport where the Airpods were bound to be cheaper. I held on and waited which rewarded me with a small discount. However, I think my waiting also taught me that although my western mind may crave immediate satisfaction, I felt more in control as I myself decided when I would fill my ears with wireless music, and no one else.

Lastly, I did think of calling this piece, 'Waiting for Podot', but I resisted. Well, until the penultimate sentence, anyway.

Karma needs a helping hand?
January 2018

I'm a libertarian. There I've said it! So, what does that mean? A friend of mine who was born early enough to experience the sixties, made a very interesting observation. He said that, 'the freedom that was so courageously fought for during that period, has mutated into something that has now back-fired. It is functionally achieving the opposite of what was originally intended'. His view is that freedom in a cohesive society is the right to choose from a selection of choices that have been mutually agreed upon. This is different from a view that freedom is the ability to choose anything one wants. That would be anarchy.

In the years since the sixties, the machinations of many civil rights organisations, and a general snowballing of the original freedom movement, have led to a society where the suppression of any personal choice is seen as a civil rights violation. Therefore, freedom has crept slowly towards extreme liberalism, the endgame of which would be anarchy. As a necessary restraint to the disruptive and divisive effects of this 'free for all', more and more regulation has been brought into force to keep the boat from capsizing. And so, well motivated non-regulation leads paradoxically to increasing regulation. It seems that paradise needs an ever increasing, and sometimes draconian, management. I believe that if an administration is too liberal, firstly, people are grateful for the liberties, then they start demanding liberties, and finally they start *taking liberties*.

So, what can be done? How can society have personal freedom, but be self-regulating without the need for gross intervention from lawmakers who may have their own political agenda? Libertarianism.

In my vision, personal freedom is balanced with personal responsibility. For example, rather than a law compelling all car occupants to wear seatbelts, the government use their considerable resources to research the injury prevention effectiveness of seatbelts. This information is made available to everyone. Finally, each car driver makes their own risk assessment of whether to wear a seatbelt or not. This passes personal responsibility to the individual. But what happens to those people who choose not to wear a seatbelt and are seriously injured as a consequence? Does society have to pay the cost of their lack of responsibility? In my view, no. The hospital bill is simply passed to the injured person. They made their personal choice, now they will have to accept the financial consequences of their decision personally.

There is an existing precedent for this system; emergency service drivers. These drivers are permitted to go through red traffic lights, no entry signs and ignore many other road regulations. But if their personal choice causes an accident, they are prosecuted as a private driver. They have a selection of professional freedoms, but their responsibility is strictly personal.

I would love to see a society where people are trusted to make their own choices. So, rather than being policed with laws and regulation, personal responsibility is focused by personal jeopardy. Society does not have to pay the price of its members' irresponsibility. That can be passed straight back to the individual, and the threat of personal jeopardy would encourage self-regulation. The system would not be perfect, but I would rather promote self-regulation, and personal consciousness, than government micro-management and the dissolving of the individual into a tightly controlled homogenous sheeplike herd.

Is it all a game?
March 2018

I guess I am not alone in sometimes wondering what the hell is going on in this world. What I mean is that for fifty-eight years I have been trying to figure-out what particular cause can be attributed to a particular effect; what exactly do I need to do to get a desired outcome. I'm still totally stumped.

There is, of course, the obvious. I drop an expensive lead-crystal glass tumbler onto the floor, it shatters. I shout obscenities at a very large, aggressive looking stranger at a football match, I get a black eye. I drive my car off of a cliff… etc. I am talking about the less obvious and infinitely more desirable things such as winning a contract, getting the girl (boy) or nailing that job. Things that can be loosely described as successful outcomes.

I was once advised that when attending a job interview, one should not try to second guess what the interviewer wants, but instead give them the best that you are. By following this strategy, you do not have to do any guessing at all. You present the honest truth of who you are, and you are either what they are looking for or you are not. If you present an untrue fabrication, you have an infinite chance of getting it wrong, and losing the job because they think you are someone other than you are. Give them the truth and you will either get the job or not, but if you gain employment you will not have to continuously live up to being someone you are not. Or worse still, trip up trying to walk in someone else's boots.

The downside to this is that so much of the outcome is in someone else's hands. You do not have control over what others do or think. And even if you lie, manipulate or cheat to influence others and the outcome, you are still swinging blindly; fate seems to operate in an unlit room and no one can see in the dark.

But it is even worse than this. Desirable outcome is not just down to other people's choices. It is down to an almost infinite malaise of circumstances such as time and place. Maybe you have heard the line, 'I'm so unlucky that even if my ship came in, I'd be waiting at the airport'.

So, it seems to me that influencing desirable outcomes is far from an exact science. Maybe it is simply foolish to believe that there is a knack that can be learnt from the myriad of online courses in anything from becoming a millionaire blogger to a self-published bestselling author. Believe me, I have tried many of the latter. In the end, I think the influence you have on fate is at best very minimal and at worst simply self-delusional.

The best we can do is two-fold; like the advice about job interviews, be honest, truthful and give one hundred percent of who you are. Secondly, be tenacious. Natural attrition is often a sad fact of life, but it is one of its hardest truths. If you last the course and are the only person left standing, you *are* the only one left standing. It's just true. As to anything else apart from the above, I think the rest is simply a game of pure chance. It may be true that, 'The more I practice, the luckier I get.'[1] But in the end, we are all at the mercy of the hand of fate and, as Blanche DuBois said, 'the kindness of strangers'.

[1] *Attributed to Gary Player, Arnold Palmer and others.*

How do you know you are you?
April 2018

"Reality is merely an illusion, albeit a very persistent one."
Albert Einstein

In my last newsletter, *Is it All a Game?*, I took a blunt stab at Karma, and tried to see if I could get fate to spill its guts. This month, I want to go further, and see if the reason it is hard to evaluate what the hell is going on in our lives, is because what we think is real, is simply an illusion.

We have all been told that we possess five senses; smell, touch, sight, hearing and taste. Some of us may know that this is not entirely true; we have many more senses than this. We have proprioception, which is the ability to know where our various body parts are in space. You rely on this when you are stopped by the police and asked to place your finger onto your nose with your eyes closed, to show you are sober. There is also equilibrioception, which gives us the ability to perceive acceleration and deceleration.

However, although many researchers now believe we have nearer to twenty-one senses, all of them are physical. They all feed back on tangible physical aspects of the world around us. Therefore, our understanding of what is *real* is solely based on our interpretation of these data. But have you ever contemplated as to who or what is getting this feedback and assessing it?

And so we come to René Descartes' famous 'mind body duality'. We seem to be a physical thing interacting with a physical world, but our consciousness appears to be something else, something non-physical. The duality is that our bodies reside in one realm while our minds appear to be in a totally different place; maybe outside of space and time. And this mind body duality persists as a barrier that we cannot seem to cross, however hard we try.

So, we find ourselves in a conundrum. Our understanding of reality can only be as good as the accuracy and quality of our physical senses, plus our minds' ability to extrapolate and fill-in the gaps in those data. At best, we are like the blind men experiencing an elephant for the first time. One blind man is feeling the elephant's trunk and so says that the animal is like a thick snake. Another is feeling the leg and says that it's more like a tree. A third feels its tusk and concludes the elephant is more like a spear. And so on.

Data can not only be misinterpreted, but can also be false. Amputees still have a sense of the limbs they no longer possess, and many suffer chronic pain from an arm or leg that was removed many years ago.

It seems undeniable that whatever our consciousness is, it is the thing that we can most closely call 'us'. It is the entity that is receiving, or at least believes it is receiving, data from a world that really exists, but this is pure assumption. That thick snake or spear or tree may actually be an elephant. Even more disconcerting for truth seekers, there may be nothing there at all; like a phantom limb.

For me, unless we find a way to eliminate the mind body separation, we have only two choices. One, we treat reality with trepidation and caution. We take a stance of high risk aversion. Two, we jump headlong into this 'reality' and immerse ourselves into it as if it is the greatest Virtual Reality game ever invented. We may 'in reality' be living a lie, but in the absence of objective truth, at least we're going to have a whole lot of fun.

I have laboured with this existential mind-bender all my life. It has been a fascinating journey, but also a frustrating one. However, there may be a route to at least partial relief from this persistent headache. I once heard the eminent quantum physicist Leonard Susskind speak about high-level mathematics as being the way he gets much nearer to understanding what *real* reality might actually look like. I suppose he believes that maths enables blind men to feel more of the elephant simultaneously, and therefore get a more accurate picture of the beast. Recently, I have been toying with the idea of studying mathematics so that I might get a glimpse of what life really is before my feeble human senses fade for ever.

What does Plato have to do with my summer shorts?
August 2018

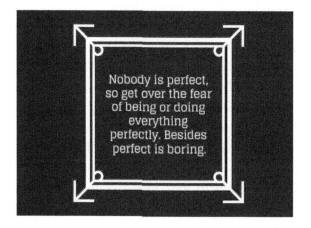

Nobody is perfect, so get over the fear of being or doing everything perfectly. Besides perfect is boring.

A couple of weeks ago, I escaped the unseasonally cold weather of Madrid for the equally unseasonal heat of the UK. This was my family's traditional two-week holiday in England. So far, so good. However, the cool summer in Spain had meant that I had not yet retrieved my shorts (or short pants) from their moth-balled hibernation. When I unpacked my case at my in-laws' in the strangely sun-drenched English town of Reading, I realised just how sad the garment had become.

I have a habit of keeping clothes for far too long - at least that is, by my other half's criterion - and my shorts, that had once been a strong and healthy khaki colour were a sad, vague green; the dull hue of over-cooked broccoli. The shape had also suffered in the repeated wear-wash cycle over the last fifteen or so years. So, my other half, Alexandra, grabbed my hand and dragged my reluctant, long-trousered self to the centre of town in search of some long-needed replacements.

I don't like shopping for clothes at the best of times, but wasting my precious English holiday trudging around the Oracle Centre in sweltering heat was definitely not high on my bucket list. After visiting Debenhams, House of Fraser, Marks & Spencer and Next, I was still short my new shorts. And this was the problem; the stores either had very limited stock or what they had was not ... well ... very nice. Everything I tried on made me look like a man old before his time or an older man trying to look much younger than physics allows. And if it wasn't that, then the pattern was ridiculous or the cut necessitated wearing the waistband nearer to my ankles than my midriff. *Universe save me*! It was at this moment that my thoughts went to Plato!

The Greek thinker proposed the philosophical theory of Idealism. His notion was that perfection can only exist in the imagination. In reality, nothing can actually be perfect; some flaws must always exist. Something or someone may get very near to perfection, but never actually perfect. Even the electron - which is the most perfectly round object in the universe - is not *perfectly* round. It is physical, Plato would say and therefore, it is flawed.

The reason I started thinking about all of this while

standing in a pile of rejected mens' shorts in a very crowded Primark, was that I had realised that I had fallen into the very human trap of expecting the impossible; I had expected *perfection*. Two hours earlier, I had set out to purchase *the* perfect pair of shorts. In my mind, I knew exactly what they would be like. The colour would counteract the excessive redness of my spindly legs; and make said spindles look muscular. The cut would make my bum look taut, as if the fabric had been stretched over "Buns of Steel" and the price would be so reasonable that I could buy a few pairs and not have to do this damned shopping thing for another fifteen years. But oh, no! Bloody Mr Plato had other ideas (ironically ideas about Idealism). The image I had held in my head was very different to reality. In my mind's eye, there existed the King of Short Trousers waiting patiently on a shelf in Reading, and like some mythical garment, they would endow me with the physique of Adonis. Reality is the pin that pops imagination's over-inflated bubble. And I could feel the wind whistling out of mine.

For half an hour I had battled with Alex. I was trying on a pair of tracksuit-style shorts. One grey with dark blue stripes and another pair with colours the other way around. Alex kept on telling me that they looked really good on me, but the pre-conceived perfect picture in my mind, would not get out of the way. But then it did. I let reality in and kicked my perfection fallacy out of the park. Suddenly I found myself saying, 'Actually, these puppies aren't too bad'. Well, I didn't really say 'puppies'. I'm not *that* cool. But having freed myself from the blinkers of a perfection drama, I returned home with two pairs of new shorts that I really like. In fact, I'm sitting here, back in Spain, wearing the little beauties as I type this newsletter!

So, the moral is; keep the idea of perfection away from reality. Perfection is very useful as an aiming spot, but don't let that impossible ideal ruin a *perfectly* good reality. Not unless you want to wear long trousers all summer.

Where there's muck, there's brass
August 2018

Have you ever heard the expression, 'Where there's muck, there's brass'? It is a saying that comes from the north of England, and is often thrown into conversations in a frivolous way, but – as Shakespeare said – 'In jest, there is truth'. It popped into my head when I was thinking about writing this month's newsletter.

The saying suggests that even in the dirtiest of pursuits, there is real value. But it could also mean that in a field that looks full of worthless muck, there are some golden nuggets.

I have been swimming, and diving deep, into the self-publishing market over the last few years, and two of the questions that keep coming up are, what makes a good book and, what elevates a particular book to bestseller status? I wondered if, 'Where there's muck, there's brass', might shed some light on this.

From the perspective of the big publishers let 'muck' read an endless sea of books, and 'brass' read cash. Might it be the case that marketeers simply look for something to sell regardless of quality, and rather than raking through the muck ourselves to discover the literary diamonds hidden there, we simply let the publishing houses tell us what's good and what's not?

What I am getting at is, are we told that a book is special, and so we start to see it as such or are there books that really *are* so special that they inexorably rise to the top? Is the publishing world a re-enactment of the Emperor's new clothes or are readers actually creating bestsellers because some books really *are* that unique?

As many of you know, I recently took a six-month writing course with the publisher Faber & Faber in London. A few weeks ago, we had a presentation of our work to literary agents. Very few of us were approached after the readings even though many of the extracts read were really very good. However, one of my classmates was approached. His extract was good. The synopsis was intriguing, but it wasn't any better than many other pieces. So, why was he one of the few that agents were interested in?

What I noticed was that his book was a dark, historical mystery set in the eighteenth century world of phrenology, where many of the other books presented were light to dark, thought provoking comedies. A day later, I was browsing the shelves of the British bookseller W. H. Smith, and there it was… All the light to dark, thought provoking comedies, like the massive bestseller *Eleanor Oliphant is Completely Fine*, had been replaced with dark thrillers like James Patterson's *The President is Missing* and John Grisham's *The Rooster Bar*. I asked a shop assistant where all the copies of *Eleanor Oliphant* had gone. 'Oh,' he said, 'they've been recalled.'

It seems that the trend had changed over night and the agents were now looking for thrillers and mysteries. They were simply following the trend and searching for something to fit neatly into it.

When an unknown writer finishes a book, the first step to traditional publication is to find an agent that likes the book and is willing to get behind it and sell it to a publisher. Therefore, agents are the people that see exactly what is being written, and are in a unique position to sift through the ocean of new writing and find the gems. But it would seem that they instead follow what the marketeers tell them is popular, and only look for that. How many wonderful books are passed over and never see the light of day. As I wrote in my book *Conversations with Eric*, '… the world is one big bushel under which many lights are hidden until they fade.'

The self-publishing market - mainly, but not exclusively, Amazon - may actually be affording readers the chance to take back their right to choose the books they want, rather than be led by commercial marketeers who may have little concern for good writing. There is no filter from agent or publisher bias on Amazon. You are presented with the full gamut of every genre and every level of writing for you to choose for yourself.

This wonderful new open marketplace is a godsend for new writers like me. But there is a huge hurdle that this system throws up; there are hundreds of thousands of us trying to be heard. Most of us are writers not salespeople, so often our calls to you may be a little crude. But I appeal to you to give us a chance, bypass the large commercial vendors that are exercising clever marketing tactics on you, the reader; take a look at the books they are not pushing down your throats, and discover your own 'brass' in the 'muck'.

When did gratitude become a dirty word?
November 2018

About a week ago, I left home with our two black labradors for the usual morning walk. My partner Alexandra was busy, so it was just me and the furry guys. I soon noticed that we kept coming across small groups of school children roaming the local countryside like packs of paranoid zombies. My first fear was that truancy had reached epidemic proportions and the end of the world was nigh, but the truth, that I found out later, filled me with much more dread. Apparently, they were on *strike*. Yes, you read that correctly; the pupils of the local school had 'downed tools' and were staging a one day strike. This walk-out was not because someone had been abused or a teacher had been wronged or Darwinism was about to be banned. No, the stated reason was that sex education was only including the *standard* male/female model. Well, I am sure that the children taking a day off to roam the Spanish countryside will definitely make the educators change their non-inclusive evil minds!

Although I whole-heartedly support the right of school children to voice grievances, they are not in a position where quasi-industrial action is even relevant let alone appropriate. As far as I understand it, workers collectively deciding to withdraw their labour as a show of universal resolve, is a human right. There is a contract between employer and worker and both sides must feel they are benefiting for the agreement to be equitable. But children have not entered into a contract. Education in Spain, as in many countries, is compulsory until the age of sixteen. Therefore, children are not entering into a voluntary contract with the school as does an employee; children are carrying out their legal obligation. Even more than this, the children are the sole beneficiaries. The state provides free education and the children consume it. It is a one-way nexus; the children are not expected to do anything for the education system as a reciprocal transaction to complete the agreement. One could argue that society benefits from the collective education of children, but the society that benefits from the current tranche of educating is in the future. Society pays it forward without any guarantee that those children will do the same when it's their turn.

I believe it is a wonderful thing that so many

societies believe it of the utmost importance to provide free education for our children, but, as I said above, although children must have a right to voice their feelings, their consumption of education is for their immediate benefit not ours; it is an act of civilised altruism on our part. I know it is not uncommon for children to naïvely believe that adult society exists solely to serve them, but it really takes the biscuit when our decency is served back to us as a cold dish of 'you call that a gift?'.

What will the proto-adults of today take with them into the future when the reins eventually come their way? If we allow this sort of behaviour we may be teaching that gratitude is not a virtue anymore; that it is okay to make demands with self-righteous foot-stamping even if the generosity of others is trampled under those solipsistic feet in the process. My position is this, if I am a starving man and am offered a sandwich by a charitable good Samaritan, I hope I would have the grace to say thank you rather than complain that it contains the wrong brand of mustard.

P.S. Our two children, Pablo and Cristina didn't even ask if they could take the day off. They knew what the answer would have been.

Luck, karma and the Jesus Delusion
January 2019

Like me, I suspect that many of you may have projects on the go that are not progressing as well as you would wish. And like me, I bet you sometimes find yourself beseeching God or the Universe for some help and a little good luck. But recently I have been questioning if the change in luck I am seeking is much nearer than I thought.

Firstly, what do we mean by 'luck'? Well, a popular definition might be;

"Success or failure apparently brought by chance rather than through one's own actions."

And I suppose that is the main snag with luck. The idea

that it is functionally outside of our control. If something is not within our control, it would be a waste of time to attempt to control it. By this simple logic we hand our lives over to fate.

A typical mindset that we use to tolerate being a cork on the sea of life and not drowning in disenfranchised misery, is to turn to karma. Karma works on the encouraging notion that Good gets rewarded and Bad punished. Hmmm! How's that one going for us?

I would suggest that the first and most powerful defence we have against the idea of luck, is cause and effect. Issac Newton put it simply with his three laws of motion. I think they apply equally well to our progression through life as an object through space. A person will keep moving forward, or stay at rest, until another force acts on them. The amount of effort a person exerts on a problem will affect the problem in proportion to the amount of force they exert and the size of the problem. And finally, every action has consequences.

The idea that things 'just happen' is simply a cop-out. What happens to us is directly influenced by what we do or do not do. I can think of only one event where a human being can claim to be totally without culpability; their own birth. Apart from that, however small the influence, we do influence everything in our lives. 'What about when other people do something to you?' I hear you cry. Well, I am not saying you always have a massive influence, but that we always have some culpability, and if we have some culpability we have some control. A person that is mugged has to be there to be mugged. If that 'victim' had taken a different route or delayed their departure by just a few seconds, they may not have been at that spot, in time and space, in the first place.

You may well think I am nitpicking and being unfair, but I am not suggesting that life is fair, just logical. To bring fairness into the equation would be to take a step backwards into the wonderful fairytale of karma, again. What I am arguing is that we always have choices, and whether we are being coerced by a bully, encouraged by a benefactor or simply pressured by the current cultural norm, *we* are the only person in control of what *we* choose to do. To blame other people for our decisions is at best a lie, and at worst to voluntarily relinquish our autonomy and hand our destiny to others.

I think the second biggest mistake we make is to go to the other extreme and believe the fate of others is in *our* hands. How often have you found yourself blaming 'bad luck' for something that has happened to you, yet in the same moment embraced personal guilt for not saving someone else? We cannot have it both ways. The only person over which we have full control is our individual self. We can make many choices to help others, but we must let them take responsibility for *their own* lives, and we must stop thinking we are responsible for their fate. Often, our desire to help others and be a decent person leads us to assume culpability for others. We are our brother's brother not their keeper. It is easy to believe that we are being good people when we make positive choices on someone else's behalf, but we actually insult their autonomy when we assume responsibility for them rather than letting them make their own decisions.

We are frail creatures in a difficult world. It is enough for us to find the strength to handle our own complicated practical and social dilemmas without taking on responsibility for the entire world. We must stop deluding ourselves that we are singularly responsible for saving mankind. If you concentrate on what you believe is the best course of action, act out of your own moral compass and make your own choices, you give to others the courtesy and freedom for them to run their own lives. Rather than driving yourself mad with guilt via a misplaced Jesus delusion, you are actually giving people ultimate respect by allowing and trusting them to stand on their own two feet, and you are taking full responsibility for standing on your own.

So, we are still stuck with 'luck'. I may make powerful self-determining choices, but I am still at the whim of luck. However, if I substitute 'serendipity' for 'luck', I suddenly feel very differently about that elusive ingredient. Serendipity as opposed to luck, refers to chance which is mathematical not unfathomable or supernatural. Mathematical chance will cause the cards to fall as they may; that is the nature of the game, but it is ruled by cause and effect, not sheer luck. Therefore, I do not have to pray or appeal to anyone. If I take control of *my* choices, I have done as much as I can. I am in charge of what I do, and serendipity is the result of the sum of all of those choices. Ultimately, I may not be able to fine tune the outcome, but I still get to choose how I play the game.

One cup of coffee = a whole novel
March 2019

In my part-time job, teaching English at Repsol I have a particular two hour class that I give a few times a week which stretches the students' brains and brings some surprising results.

The class is titled 'Personal Branding' and looks at how we see ourselves when we meet a new person, how we think others see us when we meet them for the first time and what we can do to bring these two perspectives as near to each other as possible.

The class starts with a list of questions which dig down into how we really see ourselves. How would you answer the following;

~ Is there something you wish you knew more about?

~ What's something you like to do the old-fashioned way?

~ What are some small things that make your day better?

~ What one thing do you really want, but believe you can't afford?

Strangely, (probably because I write novels) I think the first three can be answered by picking up a traditional book. Bear with me. I'm serious!

~ Is there something you wish you knew more about?

That's an easy one - It's definitely in a book, somewhere.

~ What's something you like to do the old-fashioned way?

One of the oldest and purest entertainments is reading. Rather than spending hours on Youtube, Facebook & Instagram just to stave off boredom, open a book. Your extraordinary imagination will thank you.

~ What are some small things that make your day better?

I am sure you'll have plenty of things you can name here. But as you are reading this book, I am sure that one of those things is going to be 'get stuck into a great book'. I think you might be beginning to get my drift.

And what about the last question, **What one thing do you really want, but believe you can't afford?** How regularly do we buy a coffee for a few dollars or pounds? I personally love a good cappuccino and regularly buy a Starbucks or similar when I'm out and about in Madrid. I am far from being a rich man, but allow myself the luxury of a satisfying coffee every now and then. It's only a few euros and I think I'm worth it!

But how often have I denied myself something really good that costs little more than that favourite beverage? Most eBooks cost around the same as a high-street coffee. So, a tasty hot drink and a good book cost about the same, but do they give you the same value?

If I had to make a choice between a great coffee or a great book (and in this weird scenario I can only choose one), I would have to choose the book. The choice is ten minutes of delicious pleasure or 8 hours plus of fully engaging drama, intrigue and roller-coaster emotions. The fabulous truth is that we are only talking about a few dollars for either. We live in a wonderful age when most of us can actually afford both.

So, do you fancy a good read to go with that coffee?

Intelligent Design
February 2019

Two apes are walking through a forest. One notices that the other has a pained look on his face.

"What's wrong," he asks.

"They say that humans evolved from apes, right?" replies the other ape.

"Yes, they evolved from apes. What's the problem?"

"Well, if humans evolved from apes, why are we still here?"

"Ahh," says the first ape, *"some of us had a choice."*

It is all too easy for we humans to assume that we are the top animal on the planet. After all, no other species has managed to inhabit so many diverse geographical areas, climbed to the top of the food chain or erected structures as elaborate as ours. Well, we may think that, but is it really true? We fear to tread in many inhospitable places in which bacteria thrive, and they are far older and more numerous than us. Termites build incredibly complicated and technically impressive structures, and many species use tools and have elaborate social hierarchies.

So is there anything that truly sets us apart from the other living creatures on Earth? I think there is, but it may also be the reason we are on the brink of failure.

The theory of evolution teaches us that the first forms of life were very simple. Slowly, over millions of years, slight mutations sequentially cause new species to emerge, and over eons this process lead to increasingly complicated organisms and eventually us. By the way, the opening joke is not really accurate. Humans did not evolve from apes; apes and humans have a common ancestor and we both came from that animal. That is why there are still apes as well as humans, but that's not as funny!

What seems clear to me is that biological evolution had little to do with creativity and much more to do with functionality. Creatures with DNA mutations were inevitably selected for if they produced a functional improvement. 'Thinking' played no significant part in evolution until very recently; maybe with the emergence of monkeys and apes or early hominids. Most species live only in the present. Immediate stimulus creates an automatic response, and this mechanistic routine only differs through changes in environment or mutation. However, humans think. We have the ability to imagine what might be. We can contemplate future scenarios in a way that most other animals cannot.

Biology is a little like Microsoft's Windows operating system. Slowly, over a long time, the programme was tweaked, changed and improved. Many subroutines became obsolete, but the Frankenstein monster became so complicated that no one was sure whether certain parts could be cut out or not. Furthermore, many functions had developed crazy serpentine paths that would make no logical sense if designed from scratch. A case in point for human anatomy is the *recurrent laryngeal nerve*. This nerve serves our voice box in the throat, but rather than traveling directly from the base of the brain to the throat, it sojourns down into the chest before looping around the aorta and returning back up the neck.

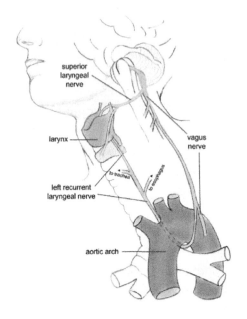

Some people disagree that this is a case of bad design, but my point is not about whether we were designed or not. I am interested in how clumsy our biology has become when seen against the astonishing advances in our thinking, technological abilities and artistic culture. Shakespeare described humans as "The beauty of the world, the paragon of animals."

Four hundred years later, with massive advances in every direction possible (think computing, space travel and communication technologies) we have advanced even more beyond our wet-work biology. If I were designing a modern human, in all its cultural, artistic and technical beauty, I would not choose frail, disease-prone biology as a suitable medium. I am not sure what material I would use, but I am worried for us. I am concerned that our minds may have outgrown our biological bodies.

Maybe it will not be nuclear war or the total breakdown of our political/social systems that will spell the end for us, but like the aliens in *War of the Worlds* it will be simple, vulnerable biology.

A year after writing this newsletter the coronavirus appeared and quickly spread across the globe. Today is 8th June 2020, and the future outcome from this pandemic is still unknown.

A metropolitan beast! Friend or foe?
March 2019

On a cold, dark morning back in early January, I found myself standing at the entrance to the Repsol Campus in Madrid. Repsol is a petroleum company that has its fingers in just about every pie into which a petro-giant can squeeze their well lubricated digits. This mega-corporation is the forth biggest company in Spain.

I was waiting for Ruth to show up and take me into the building. Ruth is a flamboyant Australian, who after many years in Spain, speaks the native language with extravagant ease, but has grammar that her countrymen would probably call 'A bit crook!'.

Why was I in the centre of Madrid at seven-fifteen a.m. on a chilly winter Tuesday? Well, I was about to embark on a new adventure to bring in a little extra money and help pay those endless bills that the postman keeps bringing; I was about to start part-time work as an English teacher and Ruth was going to be my Director of Studies.

So, there I stood in the dark, shivering in the almost sub-zero winds and a little nervous as to how I was going to cope with this new role, for which I had no formal training. As you may well know, I was an actor for some time, I have created and led a number of courses in communication and voice, and I am a writer, but could I fill the shoes of 'un profesor de inglés' as the Spanish would put it?

To stretch my nervous system even further, my first student had a reputation – a big scary one! She is the director in charge of oil trading, which for a petroleum company is a pretty important job. Her assistant is a fellow dog-walking friend of mine, and it was she that had suggested to Repsol that I would make a perfect English teacher for her boss. This was not because I had experience in teaching English, but because her boss had recently rejected two teachers in quick succession and my friend believed that my personality might well be able to tame her boss's tempestuous and demanding needs. So, no pressure, then.

The Repsol building is adorned with huge metal structures that protrude from the exterior walls like ribs, giving it the appearance of a giant mythical beast. As I stood waiting, hundreds of people swarmed towards its gaping entrance and disappeared into its depths. They looked as emotionally frozen and as miserable as I felt.

Sadness welled inside me as I looked on the Repsol building gobbling up its breakfast.

Corporate life gives me an uneasy sensation in my belly. I suppose, as a writer of conspiracy thrillers, I have a propensity to be distrustful of large companies and their gleeful consumption of us poor (literal and metaphorical) buggers for their own gluttonous enrichment. But I was so wrong. Really wrong!

I have been teaching classes at Repsol for a few weeks now and have found that the notorious director of oil trading, and indeed all the employees I rub shoulders with, are really rather lovely. The building is well appointed and conducive to a very pleasant working environment. I have no idea what the level of pay is, but it seems that the employees are very happy there. The work is varied and challenging, and the company run many classes and trainings to enhance the careers of the 4,000 staff.

I know I sound like an advert for Planet Repsol, but I am really impressed and have done a complete one hundred and eighty degree turn from my dark, weather-chilled introduction to the company a few weeks ago.

Now, you skeptics out there may well be thinking that I have been systematically drugged or programmed like a *Stepford* wife, and am not seeing the truth behind the company's disingenuous façade, but the following story may prove to uncover the truth.

One of my clients is the director in charge of all the Repsol petrol stations in Spain. He told me of an employee at the Madrid campus who was the lucky winner of the state lottery a couple of years ago. This man had already worked at a relatively ordinary job at the company for some time when he had his extraordinary stroke of luck. His winning ticket was worth €6,000,000! However, although he told his manager (my client) that he wanted to buy him a Porsche as a thank you for all his kind help over the years, and treated himself, family and friends to some wonderful gifts, he stayed at the company in his regular job. To me, that speaks volumes. Either this man is an idiot or Repsol really is as good a place to work as it looks.

As for me, I am loving it. I get to spend hours every week with some really nice and interesting people, basically chatting. I still hate the bitterly cold mornings, but feel very lucky to be earning a few quid doing a very enjoyable job.

What are you bonded with?
April 2019

I, like many people I have known and loved, suffer with depression. Over many years, I have come to understand that depression often comes from a feeling of loneliness; a feeling of isolation. If you have fallen foul of this 'Black Dog' as Winston Churchill referred to his dark moods, then you may well recognise the feeling of being totally on your own in a world that neither cares about you, needs you or loves you.

It is not *unusual* for depressives to turn to addictive behaviours in a desperate attempt to dull the pain; to fill the void, to go to extremes to connect with something… anything. This may take the shape of an obsessive antisocial habit, alcoholism or drug addiction. None of this is news to most of us, but when I came across a TED

Talk video of Johann Hari, my understanding of the problem changed completely.

https://youtu.be/PY9DcIMGxMs
(Please try the above, but note that this link may no longer be available)

What Hari explains from his research is that we have totally misunderstood what addiction is, but more importantly, why it happens. He believes that it is all about our fundamental need for bonding. The common understanding of addiction came partly from a series of experiments with rats. A rat was put into a cage with two water bottles. One contained water and the other cocaine laced water. Within a very short amount of time, the rat began to obsessively drink the cocaine water until it finally died. This was always taken as proof positive that a propensity to addiction was innate and we are all a small slip away from this evil road to ruin.

But when another scientist decided to test this experiment a little further he found the real reason for the rat's self-destructive behaviour. He placed a test rat in a rat Shangri-La. It was a spacious cage full with everything a rat could want including many other rats that the test subject could play and procreate with to its heart's content. The rat barely touched the cocaine water, preferring to entertain itself with the many playthings and fellow rodents. It was concluded that if the rat was isolated and had nothing to connect with, it would bond with the drug. But in an environment of many positive things, the rat chose a healthy life.

It would appear that we need to bond with something to maintain our mental health. For most of us that will be another person, but it could be a profession, a pet or a social cause. If circumstances do not allow or provide us with a life affirming choice, in desperation we will bond with anything. Johann Hari suggests that our age old method of getting people off of addictions with stern punishment is both cruel and totally ineffective. These people are suffering from a lack of a positive bond, so prohibiting what they have bonded with will force them to choose something else and that may be as bad or worse than their original choice. What we need to do is give them something positive to bond with, then wean them off of the destructive addiction. Hari concludes that "the opposite of addiction is not sobriety, the opposite of addiction is connection."

So, here is a very challenging question: What are you most bonded with? If you find that it is something healthy, then that is great, but this simple question may expose a fundamental truth that is at the heart of a darkness that has plagued you for years. Maybe you will find that it is not something terrible at all, but in the cold light of day it is not as attractive as you hoped. If that is you, you can cast your eye around and find something that you are much happier with. The important thing is that you become aware that if something has felt amiss in your life, this ridiculous little question may hold the key. And more excitingly, you get to choose what is important in your life, and can consciously decide what you bond with.

Smile, cry and keep on going
April 2019

I have been asked to write an article for the writers' circle I used to attend when I was in England. I thought you might enjoy it also. They are about to celebrate 65 years of existence. That's got to be some sort of record!

Why do we do anything? No, really. Why do you go to work, brush your teeth or even get out of bed in the morning?

I am a great believer in the notion that our emotions and our minds, although intricately linked, are two separate tools which must be employed correctly if we don't want to find ourselves bashing home a delicate screw with a lump hammer. For me, it is our minds that are the practical enablers; the clever hard-working dispassionate experts that dream our dreams and then find practical ways to achieve them. On the other hand, our emotions are terrible planners and even worse decision makers. It is our intellects that are the do-ers. But it is our emotions that make the whole confusing, painful, awesome, miraculous journey worthwhile simply by enjoying the ride.

So, how does the mind work? Well, I'm using mine right now writing this piece. I can feel ideas churning away inside my head. But they aren't random, they are focused. The mind is a precision tool used to find a tidy, efficient path from A to B or to get a particular job done. My current task is to write something about life, the art of writing and in particular the *Verulam Writers' Circle* who have been instrumental in helping me develop from a writer who *wants* to write to one that actually *does*. But although it is my mind that is pecking away at the keyboard, employing thousands of years of evolved syntax and grammar and actually coming up with the ideas I am trying to convey, none of this would happen if something deep inside me didn't *feel* it worthwhile.

Every idea I have ever had has come from my mind. Ideas are practical, tangible and logical. An impractical or illogical idea is not a lot of use to anyone. Emotions, on the other hand, are not necessarily the opposite, but they are pure joy, pain or simply a self-sustaining feeling of wellbeing.

Every time we do something there is a motivation behind it; a force as real as the physical forces that beat at the heart of Newtonian mechanics. That motivation is driven by either something we want to do or something we feel we should do. Either way, we do things because we get a tangible reward; a rush of emotion, feel-good feedback that has evolved to keep us moving forwards. It is the force that has brought us from bland single-cells to what Shakespeare called, 'the paragon of animals'.

I once heard it said that, 'We read to know we are not alone.' We are islands of ideas in seas of emotion. Our words, whether written or spoken, are the frail boats that connect us and it is the pure joy of sailing that makes us all such purposeful mariners. Without the sometimes stormy, sometimes mirror smooth seas we would be ideas without a purpose.

I joined the Verulam Writers' Circle to be with other people who felt, like me, that they had a precious cargo of ideas and knew that those musings would have no purpose unless we could find a way to share them with others. For most of us, fame and fortune would not be the reward, and even for the fortunate few who would succeed in making a living from writing, the real reward is always facing your fears and diving into that capricious sea of emotion that links each of us to all of us.

Why do I get out of bed in the morning? Because I have weird and wonderful thoughts, and I love sharing them with the other extraordinary islanders around me. And when I have the courage to do so, it is my emotions that make me smile, cry and want to keep on going.

The head is where the heart is
June 2019

Can you be satisfied with whatever life throws at you? Well, Dan Gilbert of Harvard university believes that we do not need to chase happiness. He thinks we already have everything we need to achieve it.

In times gone by, we used to think that happiness resided in our hearts. But even though modern science has proved that our emotions come from our brains rather than that stalwart pump, we still tend to feel that happy emotions are something separate from the cold logical workings of our minds. However, a lot of research like the studies done by Dan Gilbert, suggest

Paul Casselle

that happiness can be manufactured in our brains regardless of what is actually happening in our lives. There's an old story that goes like this;

Two young boys take part in an experiment. The first boy is led to a room that is wall to wall with every kind of toy and video game a young teenager could ever want. The second boy is taken to a room that is waist deep in horse shit. The boys are left in their respective rooms for a number of hours.

When the psychologists return, they find that the first boy has destroyed all the toys and is sitting in the middle of mounds of debris with an angry look on his face.

"What's the problem?" they ask. "Why have you broken all the toys?"

He turns to them with hatred in his eyes. "None of the toys are the right colour, the video games are not the most up to date and I had to wait a whole twenty seconds for this stupid internet to download each new level."

The scientist write on their clipboards, then move on to the second room.

They open the door and look around. The room is totally empty apart from the copious amounts of manure. Suddenly a smiling head appears above the smelly sludge, but quickly ducks down again into the brown sea. A moment later, the grinning head pops up a second time. The scientists call out to the boy, but no sooner has he waved a joyful hello, than he plummets out of sight again.

On his third appearance, the lead scientist shouts loudly.

"Stop!"

The boy pauses, doggy-paddling to keep his head above the brown, aromatic ocean.

"What are you doing?" says the scientist. "And why are you so happy?"

The boy beams pure joy. "With all this horse shit," he says with a glint in his eye, "there must be a pony in here somewhere!"

It appears that the problem is mostly down to excessive choice which leads to inflated expectations. Once we have an idea of what will make us happy, our ability to actually be happy becomes totally dependent on that specific outcome. Anything else will be an inevitable 'bummer'.

The first boy is spoilt for choice. Now, whatever toy he plays with sets his mind thinking about whether he has made the right selection. It doesn't matter which toy he picks up, there will always be many more he is neglecting, and one of those may be a better choice. The second boy is denied a range of things to choose from. He only has a room full of manure. According to the conclusions of Gilbert, this engages the unique ability we humans have to manufacture happiness from the situation we actually have and cannot change.

Gilbert gives a funny example of this. He says that if you are on a first date and you notice that the other person regularly picks their nose, this may well be the end of that potential romance. But if you are married to that person and they pick their nose habitually, it is much harder to reject the entire relationship. You are invested and much more likely to search for sanguinity by saying, 'Well, they have a heart of gold, but don't touch the fruit cake.'

A few weeks ago, I asked you to vote on which of four books you'd like me to work on next. Did I do the right thing? When I produce the book most of you voted for, will you worry that you asked for the wrong book and another title would have been better?

One of my readers emailed me and said that I should write the book I feel most passionate about and that would always be the best choice. Writing the book the majority said they wanted will always leave those who *didn't* vote for *that* title dissatisfied and the ones that get the book they voted for wondering if they made the best choice. It makes me think of Abraham Lincoln's adage;

"You can please *all* of the people *some* of the time and *some* of the people *all* of the time, but you can't please *all* of the people *all* of the time."

Lincoln was talking about an individual making the right choice regarding others, and my book survey was the same; what book do my readers want. But maybe this is missing the point. Maybe happiness is not about pleasing others, but about being happy with the outcome we get. Should we concentrate on being content with whatever actually happens rather than fixating on preferred outcomes. Can we choose to be happy with what we get rather than allowing ourselves to be unhappy for *not* getting what we want?

Some of you know that my office is a windowless room in my basement. When I moved into this house and discovered that it was the only feasible place for me to set up shop, I had a terrible time coming to terms with that reality. But now, many novels and newsletters later, I find it hard to write anywhere else. I actually love my funny little room.

It seems that we may all be fighting to get something we already have. It is said that beauty is in the eye of the beholder. Maybe happiness is in the *mind* of the beholder.

Here's hoping!
July 2019

Franz Kafka is often quoted as saying, 'There is hope, but not for us.' This is a rather depressing conclusion. So, I thought I would take a personal look and decide for myself.

The evidence

Three days a week I travel to Repsol HQ to teach English, doing my bit to perfect the language skills of their four thousand employees. I reach central Madrid by way of bus and Metro with the journey taking a bone-jiggling two hours.

A couple of things were very noticeable from the moment I started my tri-weekly commute. The first was the super human effort that people exhibited to achieve the total avoidance of acknowledging that anyone else exists. Now, I am very conversant with travelling around London on public transport so, the hysterical evasion of eye contact was not new to me. However, this was something different. People seemed completely devoid of the many mannerisms that help me to differentiate a fellow human being from say, a hat-stand. Three times a week I feel like an extra on the set of a zombie apocalypse movie.

The second thing I noticed was that a huge proportion of averted gazes were fixed on mobile phones clasped in white-knuckled fists. I was left with an uncomfortable feeling. Had I missed the memo that informed us that digital, simulated social interaction must be selected when there is even the *slightest* chance that a real-life person might actually speak to you?

These two rather shocking behaviours lead to a third upsetting consequence. As a veteran of the London Underground, I have been indoctrinated into certain protocols learnt while travelling many hundreds of miles beneath the streets of the capital. Without exception, passengers wanting to board a train wait patiently for the onboard commuters to disembark first. This is not only good manners, it is the only action that is logical. You would not attempt to move into a hotel room while the previous occupant is still in the process of emptying the wardrobe, and I have never witnessed anyone forcing a second slice of bread into a toaster before removing the recently browned slice first. As I say, logic. Maybe the zombie swarm that inhabit the subterranean tunnels of Madrid have consumed one too many *tweets* or been vacuously *liked* into a trance.

No such protocol on the Madrid Metro

As an approaching train rattles into the station, the empty vessels of humanity puddle around the carriage doors holding onto their smartphones with more determination than they have for life itself. The doors slide open and a passenger or two escape before the waiting zombies push, head-strong and eyes down, onto the tightly packed train without any regard for the exiting passengers. Collateral damage is usually only toes crushed underfoot, but if this keeps up I may not be able to hold back from waging full-on, elbows-up war.

I observe their distinct lack of environmental awareness with great sadness because I am one of those annoying people who chats to strangers on buses, in cinema queues and during those four hour delays at the airport. Rather than finding my fellow travellers irritating (although to tell the truth I could kill some of them) I actually enjoy talking to people and get a buzz from simply being pleasant. I probably piss-off the odd passenger at times, but I believe that society is a collection of interacting people rather than a loose assortment of autonomous bumper-cars.

There seems to be a growing tide of solipsistic behaviour as people strive to live lives unencumbered by the need to consider anyone else. The human desire to interact with others is fast being replaced with a virtual world of streamed banality beamed to hand-held mobile devices. I watch people scrolling through a blur of images, only stopping when a shiny thing catches their eye. Like a flock of lobotomised magpies, we flit from one thing to another, not because these things are useful, but because they shine brighter than the last selfie or photograph of someone's lunch or a cat that looks extraordinarily like Marilyn Monroe. Was Kafka right? Is there no hope for us?

Then *this* happened last week

I got onto my usual Metro train which was crowded to the point that I could not even find a hand-rail to lean against let alone a seat. I moved across the carriage to the double doors on the other side and propped myself against the door. A passenger to my right caught my eye. This was surprising as not only was he actually looking at me, he asked me if I would like to take his place which was a solid bulkhead rather than a flimsy door. Now, this had happened a few weeks earlier and had rather shocked me. I am well aware that I am about to turn sixty, but I do not believe that I look frail enough to be offered preferential treatment. Moreover, that incident also marked an unwelcome milestone in my life as it was the first time that I had been offered a seat. However, this second time felt different. The person suggesting that I take his place had an energy about him that I can only describe as, human. The offer did not have the dubious odour of good manners, but was full of warmth and genuine decency by way of a sincere smile. I thanked him, but did not exchange places with him as mine was the next stop, but I was left moved by his kindness.

What seems very significant to me is that he was a young teenager. If there is any hope for us it will be reflected in the generation-in-waiting. If society's future rests in the hands of the worlds media obsessed zombies, I think Kafka may probably have hit the nail on the head. However, if that young commuter is indicative of what is around the next corner, I believe we may well make it.

The following is some text that was deleted from the original newsletter above. I am including it as I think it makes some additional points that you may find interesting.

Many people are surprised to hear that during the winter months, central Spain is held in an icy grasp. So, I bundle myself up with as many clothes as I can manage while still being able to squeeze myself into a Metro carriage. Conversely, in the summer Madrid's temperature soars and the reverse becomes true. I wear as little as is decent for a man fast approaching his sixtieth birthday. However, one thing remains constant, though. Ninety percent of my fellow commuters would not notice if I was dressed in the blood-soaked hide of a recently deceased *toro* from a local bull ring or travelled in pink nakedness wearing nothing but a pair of Crocks, as all their eyes are glued to their mobile phones.

The reason that I think it is better to talk to strangers instead of solipsistically burying your face in social media, is that the former is productive and the latter consumptive. Put simply, productive behaviour adds value to the world by creating assets and commodities, while consumption depletes those same items. We need both of course, but in order to enjoy consumption we must first produce. That is obvious.

However, I would say that more than just balancing the IN/OUT ledger, all lasting spiritual fulfilment comes only from production.

Many people would prefer to watch sport more regularly than play it, or go to a movie rather than make one, and a lot of people would argue that they derive great pleasure from this consumption. I agree, I love watching television, eating in restaurants and having lazy days, but I believe that a need to produce is in our fundamental makeup, and if we only consume we become lethargic and depressed.

Is the solution worse than the problem?
July 2019

Some years ago, I remember meeting a young woman at a party who worked in a high street jewellery shop. When I asked her what that was like she answered with the following;

"The job's okay. The money ain't bad, I like my workmates and the shop's only ten minute's walk from my house. If it wasn't for the f**king customers it'd be perfect!"

So, the solution to this person's woes would be no customers. But that would also make the job a useless pursuit in itself. A solution is no solution if it destroys the very thing it was trying to solve for in the first place. A solution must be both feasible and helpful. If the baby gets thrown out with the bathwater… well, I am sure you get my drift.

Speak no evil, see no evil, hear no evil

Maybe one of the problems is that many situations that need correction are zero-sum. We live in a finite universe, so as you correct one thing you consequently make something else worse. As you move in one righteous direction you end up further from all other points. It is *impossible* to get everything right. Therefore, every solution becomes a compromise; often having to choose the lessor of a number of evils. But as someone once remarked, 'If you choose the lesser of two evils you are still choosing evil.'

I remember an event when I was a very young boy. I had saved for some time to buy a particular toy from a shop at the end of our street. When sufficient money had finally been accumulated, I marched triumphantly down to the shop to find that they had only one of the prized items left in stock. That was okay; I only wanted one. However, after inspecting the toy I found a small blemish on its pristine plastic. It was purely cosmetic, but rendered the item *imperfect*. They offered the foot-stamping child the only two options available; a discount for the slightly marred product or a perfect specimen when new stock arrived in two weeks time. After a lot of wailing and mutterings of, 'it's so unfair', I left the establishment empty-handed. I had chosen to erase the existence of the toy from my mind rather than deal with disappointment.

Let's break it down

So what is the solution to this conundrum? Okay, let's break it down and see if we can find an answer. Firstly, I would suggest that there are two types of problems; perfect and imperfect. A *perfect* problem is quantifiable and has a single absolute solution. For example, I want to buy something for £10, but only have £9. Solution; I need an extra pound. There are a number of possible actions that could be taken; I could ask for a 10% discount, I could steal the item or I could simply kill the shop assistant (on occasions I have been confronted with some exceptionally difficult people and this thought fleetingly crossed my mind), but that would be going way beyond what is necessary. The problem is simply a lack of a single pound. Whereas an *imperfect* problem is when I want to buy something for £10 and I have the £10, but the item is no longer available. Now I have to find out if the item will be available again (and have to wait) or search for a second hand one or choose an alternative. Imperfect problems require choosing from less than perfect solutions, and therein lies the difficulty; accepting something that is less than perfect.

So, with the above in mind it would seem that the real problem is dealing with the disappointment of settling for something that is less than perfect.

Back to the toy store...

The decision I made in a toy shop more than fifty years ago has become a touchstone for me whenever I have to face an imperfect problem. Life rarely brings forth exactly what we are looking for. We would be much more content if *we could want what we have* rather than insisting *we have what we want*. What I know now, that sadly no child does, is that most of human life is a series of imperfect problems. True perfection is an ideal that only exists in the imagination. In the real world everything is imperfect. Once we learn to accept that, a small mark on the side of a toy disappears under the avalanche of joy derived from hours of playing with a prized purchase that is as perfect as our inventive minds wants it to be.

How to swallow a large frog
August 2019

It has been said that if you have to swallow a frog, don't think about it first. And if you have to swallow more than one frog, start with the largest. This newsletter is about my biggest current frog and how I am attempting to swallow it.

Starting early

When I was a boy, dreaming my naïve dreams about a world that was still an exciting mystery to me, I wanted to be an artist. I didn't totally understand the term, but

I liked it. I believed it was something to do with feeling big emotions and expressing them poetically. For example, one could say 'I love you' – subject, verb, object – which conveys the message simply and functionally, but poetry goes so much further. It evokes emotion as well as function (and sometimes leaves function out completely). Look at how Shakespeare took the sentiment 'I love you' and finessed it into his sonnet number 18 'Shall I compare thee to a summer's day? Thou art more lovely and more temperate…'. 'Poetry (is) the employment of far more words than necessary, to express ideas that fewer could not.' (*Conversations with Eric*).

My career meandered in various directions until I finally embarked on my first truly artistic pursuit; acting. From my early twenties to my mid-thirties, I battled my way through a sea of theatrical agents and a desert of terrible acting jobs. However, there were some wonderfully high points like my *very* first television appearance in 1990, billed as 'Policeman at Hospital', in a very expensive BBC wartime drama where I was treated like royalty and paid a King's ransom, and a nationwide theatre tour of Pilgrim's Progress playing the title role of Christian. I remember with dubious pride that *The Times Literary Supplement* called my performance 'an immaculate conception'.

To be, or not to be

However, at this point, more than ten years from the moment that I had first pranced onto a spotlit stage, I became aware that the lights had become intolerably dim. I came face to face with my first really big frog. In my dramatic way I saw it as a 'to be, or not to be' moment. I still loved acting, but two important things were missing. One, I was spending more time 'resting' than acting; and two, I was earning far too little from acting jobs to sustain even basic subsistence. I needed to make a decision. I needed to be realistic about how my chosen profession was working out. I needed to find another path. I needed to wake up and smell the coffee, face the music and swallow that damned frog!

I did dispatch that croaking dilemma. It was difficult, but even decades later it still looks like the most logical decision I could have made at the time. This does not mean it was the best decision, it simply means that with hindsight it continues to look like a decent one, and most importantly, a choice that helped me to push forward in a positive way.

I moved onto various artistic pursuits and did all I could to give them my best shot, but as so many of us find, when we reach out for our dreams, they often manifest as frogs rather than princes. As each of those life choices crept past their 'sell by' dates, down the hatch they went, after painful and careful deliberation. And so we arrive at my present artistic incarnation with quill in hand and a short string of books bearing my name. But after five years of modest progress, I fear I hear a familiar croaking in the wings.

D.I.Y?

As many of you know I am self-published, which means I do everything from writing my books to advertising and distributing them. However, what I have strived for is to find a literary agent who will work on my behalf to get me a publishing deal. That has always been my goal, as I am pretty sure I can write a decent book, but even surer that I am *crap* at marketing. I have worked hard, long and sometimes cleverly at recruiting an agent; however getting these overstretched people to even look at the opening chapters from one of my books has proven to be virtually impossible up to now. So, as the croaking grows louder, I am faced with a serious decision yet again.

Currently, I am teaching English in Madrid three days a week. The other two days (and some weekends, when I have the energy) are reserved for writing. However, the best laid plans of mice and men, and all that! The truth is that I have not managed to write very much recently. When I allow myself to be totally honest about the situation, I realise that the only thing that kept me pushing forward in the past was that writing was the only job I did professionally, and my diminishing savings kept me afloat. All my energies and mental capacities could pour onto my pages and I managed to produce a number of passable novels. But now I am spending long hours teaching and the bills are beginning to tower over my finances. As much as I have tried to 'box clever', I simply do not have the strength to do everything and money worries are securing the last nails into my ability to get down and write.

The Solution
There is often a way out of hell, but it is seldom painless.

This one is proving to be no exception. I have decided to hang up my writing clogs for the time being and start teaching full-time. By doing this, I will reduce the debilitating pressure I have been feeling and increase my income to a liveable level. I will also be in a better mental state to renew my battle with the world of literary agent-*ing*. My short term aim is to give this plan one hundred percent commitment for a year. When the dust settles in twelve months time, I will take another look at what would be the best next move. In the meantime, I will keep sending my monthly newsletters to stay in touch with you, and hope you will also continue to write to me. I love hearing from all of you.

Please keep supporting me

A consequence of this plan is that I will probably not have any new books for you in the near future. However, it is really important to me that you know that I am seriously grateful to all of you for buying my books, sending me some great emails and leaving wonderful reviews on Amazon. Please do not think I am abandoning my side of this deal. I am taking the most supportive action I can think of to get me into a position where I can write new books for you. If I carry on as I have been, I think there will be no winners at all.

So there it is. Life throws me another challenge and I have re-grouped. And I am ready for it. They say 'it ain't over till the fat lady sings'. Well, I am not hearing any singing at the moment, just faint croaking, and I have proven to myself many times over the years that I can deal with that. It simply takes commitment, willpower and a big frog-flavoured gulp!

How to fly without wings!
September 2019

I told you in a previous newsletter that I was taking a break from writing so that I could devote more time to teaching English and making some much-needed money. To aid my mobility between teaching appointments, I have bought myself a motorbike. Although I spent many years buzzing around the streets of London on two wheels, that was more than thirty years ago – yeah! – three-0 years ago! My shiny new (new to me - it's a 2007 model) motorbike arrives next week and I am a little trepidatious. I am praying that my nearly sixty year-old mind and body will remember how to wrestle the 500cc beast.

Keep on learning...

To help, I have been watching a lot of videos on Youtube and although long-unused neurones are beginning to vaguely recall my past skills, there is also some new stuff as well. One thing that seems to be a very popular subject at the moment is 'counter steering'. This, like so many things in life, is totally counter intuitive. The technique gets the bike to turn quickly, and involves pushing hard on the handlebar to make the vehicle lean to the side (and therefore turn) instantly. The weird thing is that you push the left-hand side to turn left and the right to turn right. This means that the front wheel points in the direction opposite to the one in which you wanted to go. At speeds above twenty mph, it is apparently the angle of lean that steers rather than the direction of the front wheel. Yup, it makes my head hurt as well.

I am not unfamiliar with counter intuitive practices. There is the acroplane safety procedure of putting on one's own oxygen mask before attending to children (an asphyxiated adult is no help to anyone) and the time-old classic of 'more haste, less speed'.

It seems to me that even if a method looks wrong or seems unnecessarily dangerous, in truth it may be the best choice.

Simple, but spot-on

There is a poem by Christopher Logue that many of you

may know. It suggests that there may be powers at work that are hard for us to acknowledge.

> *"Come to the edge," he said.*
> *"We're comfortable back here," they said.*
> *"Come to the edge," he said.*
> *"We're too busy," they said.*
> *"Come to the edge," he said.*
> *"It's too high," they said.*
> *"Come to the edge," he said.*
> *"We're afraid," they said.*
> *"Come to the edge," he said.*
> *"We'll fall," they said.*
> *"Come to the edge," he said.*
> *And they did.*
> *And he pushed them.*
> *And they flew.*

When I first read the poem I cried. I so often let my lack of trust in the universe get in my way. Every time I re-read it, the same mix of emotions tug at my eyelids. It is a simple message that if we face our fears we may well find that we fly rather than plummet. But how can we know whether our imagination is just taking our rational fears and manifesting them as a potential danger that is not actually there, or if a sheer drop really does lie around the next bend rather than a life-affirming revelation? The short answer is that we *cannot* know for sure. Sometimes we simply need to take the plunge and leave the outcome to providence.

A few years ago, I heard a joke that pokes fun at the power of providence. In 1934, a Yorkshire factory worker, Percy Shaw, invented a device that has made road travel immeasurably safer for the whole world. His invention was the reflective road stud known as the 'Cat's Eye'. An often-told story reports that the idea came to him when he was driving home one particularly dark night and managed to avoid running off of the road due to his car's headlights being reflected back at him by a cat that was sitting on the crash barrier, turning and looking in his direction. Providence indeed! However, someone once joked that had the cat turned around, tail in the air, and walked away from him, he would have invented the pencil sharpener!

All joking aside, we cannot second-guess providence, but we may be able to give ourselves more of a chance in life if we simply give in to that fact, push on that handlebar, slow down rather than rush, and take a risk or two. Maybe rather than crashing and burning, we'll find ourselves flying.

Choices!
December 2019

As many of you will know, I have had to make a number of important choices lately. Decisions are sometimes easy, but as we slide down time's inexorable slope, we discover that this is not *always* the case. I often try to be comforted by the well-known prayer written by Reinhold Niebuhr;

> *God, grant me the serenity to accept the things I cannot change,*
> *Courage to change the things I can,*
> *And wisdom to know the difference.*

Unfortunately, although this prayer's simplicity is breathtaking, the underlying challenge it makes to each of us is monumental. As if it is not difficult enough to live by the first two instructions and find super human levels of serenity and courage, we are also asked to know when to apply each.

The problem is further compounded by the fact that choices have consequences, and can lead to both good or dire outcomes. In that precise moment when we need to make a choice, we are also required to make an educated guess as to what the outcome will be. We need to foretell the future. A very difficult challenge. Someone once said that the future is very difficult to predict, especially in advance. Maybe I will find a crystal ball in my stocking this Christmas, but failing that, I will need to move ahead making choices with my fingers tightly crossed behind my back.

And so it was for Tsutomu Yamaguchi, a Japanese engineer with Mitsubishi. On 6th August 1945, he was concluding a three-month-long business trip. Yamaguchi was making his way to the train station in central Hiroshima to return to his home city some 450km away. At 8:15am, the American bomber the *Enola Gay* dropped its cargo, the world's first atomic bomb named *Little Boy*, three kilometres from where Yamaguchi was standing.

The explosion ruptured the man's eardrums, temporarily blinded him and left him with serious burns over one side of the top half of his body. After recovering, he crawled to a shelter and, having rested, he set out to find his colleagues. They had also survived and together they spent the night in an air-raid shelter before returning to Nagasaki the following day. A few days later, having had treatment for his wounds and being heavily bandaged, he reported for work.

At 11:00am on 9th August, Yamaguchi was describing the blast in Hiroshima to his supervisor, when the American bomber *Bockscar* dropped the *Fat Man* atomic bomb over the city. He was again three kilometres from ground zero, but this time he was unhurt by the explosion.

You might conclude that Yamaguchi was an extremely *unlucky* man, but on the other hand, he did survive two atomic bombs and lived to see the year 2010, dying at the age of ninety-three.

Whatever we may think, the future will always be unknowable. As much as we like to believe that our carefully chosen set of lottery numbers has more chance of winning than any other set, serendipity is driven by statistics not human desire. We know that the chances of being the UK lottery winner is one in fourteen million, someone wins most weeks, but before those balls are picked out, we can never know *who* that "one" will be. To believe we can out-smart fate is simply hubris. The best we are able to do is make the most responsible decisions we can based on the best information available at that moment.

I cannot know if taking a year off writing will turn out to be the best decision, but I am making a decisive choice. The rest... well, we will find out next year.

I will leave you with one of my favourite parables. It's an ancient Arabian tale that very entertainingly shows the folly of second-guessing the future.

A merchant in Baghdad sent his servant to the marketplace for provisions. Soon afterwards, the servant came home white and trembling and told him that while in the marketplace he was jostled by a woman whom he recognised as Death. She looked at him and made a threatening gesture. Borrowing the merchant's horse, he fled at great speed to Samarra, a distance of about seventy-five miles, where he believed Death would not find him. Intrigued, the merchant went to the marketplace himself and found Death. He asked why she had made the threatening gesture to his servant. She looked at him quizzically and said,

"That wasn't a threatening gesture, it was a start of surprise. I was astonished to see him in Baghdad as I have an appointment with him tonight in Samarra."

Try not to be a ****!
December 2019

> # Never let bad people stop you from being a good person.

There aren't many thoughts in my head when my alarm goes off at 5AM, but one of those scarce bedfellows is: how do I find a compelling reason to struggle from beneath the warm comfort of soft sheets to stand naked in the lightless morning frigidity of my bedroom? As much as I may wish there was, there is no getting away from the fact that even after I achieve the near impossible and lever myself from the unchallenging bliss of my bed, that will not be the end of the torture. The next one and a half hours will be a non-stop procession of bare-fleshed to clothed preparation until I finally don my motorbike gear and head off into the dark, windy and single-digit temperatures outside. Yes, even the Madrid area is a frozen wasteland at this time of year.

So why am I telling you this? Am I attempting a 'bird feigning a broken wing' ruse to draw in sympathy? Or am I just indulging in that favourite of British pastimes, moaning! (thought sidebar - is the act of moaning simply secular praying?). Actually, I am trying to introduce the subject of being a good person by making good choices. In my last newsletter I talked about the need to make choices rather than let yourself be a cork at sea; powerless and at the whim of life's foibles. This time I want to think about the type of person our choices make us.

The 'evil that we do' – whether it is using the last of the milk for a large bowl of cereal even though you know the rest of the family will be getting up soon and be gasping for a cuppa, or screaming at an annoying child in the supermarket that, 'there is no bloody Father Christmas, anyway' to purposely running over your neighbour's cat because you are angry with your spouse – comes from a lack of personal control rather than an absence of morals. What I am saying is that we all know right from wrong, we just have trouble overcoming the petulant, self-centred child inside us.

We also have the problem of being so short-sighted that we unwittingly become hypocrites. You may know the story of the young father helping his son with his homework. The father notices his son using a pen that he doesn't recognise.

"Where did you get that pen?" he asks.
"I borrowed it from a kid at school," the boy answers.
"But you didn't give it back," continues the father. *"If you*

keep something that isn't yours, whatever the situation, that's theft!"

The boy looks appropriately admonished. The father continues,

"If you need a pen, just ask me and I'll take one from work."

One of my favourite comedians is the Australian Jim Jeffries. If you do not know him, I introduce the loud-mouthed Aussie with a warning; his language is just about the foulest it is possible to be, and he shoots straight from the hip. If you search for him on Youtube, you do so at your own risk!

Jeffries performed a famous piece about how the Ten Commandments are held up as a template for being a righteous person. He points out that none of the instructions are much more than the common sense of decency and that we really do not need to be handed such basic information to be good people. He boils it down to a very simple commandment that I find impossible to disagree with. We all get it wrong from time to time, that is totally okay. We are human. We make errors of judgement or simply momentarily let ourselves down. We know what bad behaviour is. None of us need to be told not to commit murder, lie or steal. But I think we would instantly create a better society if we took Jeffries' commandment to heart.

So, this Christmas, in the words of Jim Jeffries, simply, 'try not to be a ****!'

Until next time, have a happy Christmas and a new year full of great choices, Paul

P.S. If you don't mind bad language and want a Christmas laugh, take a look at *Fascinating Aida's* seasonal song;

https://youtu.be/JmoG4JY_T58
(Please try this link, however, I cannot guarantee that it will still be active)

Your hidden talents - This may surprise you!
May 2020

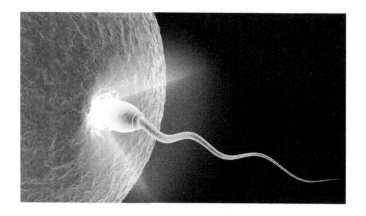

You may be reading this and thinking that you are an average person, that there is nothing special about you. If you *are* thinking something like this, I believe you are very wrong.

We can all think of people that we admire as being great humans. One of my heroes is Steve Jobs. He believed in better and set out to create the best computer experience he could for the man in the street. He didn't focus on money or power, but doggedly kept his eye on the pursuit of excellence in the field in which he had extraordinary talent. However, although Steve Jobs was spectacular, Bill Gates, who did something very similar in the same industry, is a more impressive human. Why? Let me start at the beginning.

The existence of each of us is statistically impossible. But I am here reading these words, I hear you say, so that must be nonsense. Okay, consider this. We are the offspring of two parents, four grandparents, eight great-grandparents and so on. In just nineteen generations this means that each of our ancestral trees consists of 1,048,576 people. Go back another ten generations and the number of ancestors has grown to over a billion people. Travel back just another ten generations and your forebears now number over one trillion (thought sidebar - many of our ancestors are shared).

Now imagine that each new generation is the totally unique coupling of two strangers with the female giving, at random, just one of her 300,000 eggs and the man providing a single sperm from a potential 40 million in a single ejaculation. And in every single one of those millions of couplings in your past, a specific egg had to be fertilised by a particular sperm or you would have been someone different. But you are you. And the odds of you being you in particular are ridiculously slim. Every one of us is a mathematical miracle.

Our personalities and talents emerge from a mixture of the attributes of our parents and the genetic propensities of their parents before them, and we all have the potential to exhibit both the helpful and unhelpful traits from all of our millions of ancestors. Therefore, the chances are very high that we will have unique or at least very useful abilities. It is highly unlikely that any one of us will have no talent at all.

With all of this in mind, maybe like me, as you sit in *coronavirus* isolation considering how extraordinarily fortunate you are to exist at all, you might start to contemplate what attributes you have accumulated from all the trillions of people that met, mated and led to you. If we could tap into those abilities, and have a little good fortune, we all have a chance to create something wonderful. And those that manage to do this may become wealthy and influential.

Money[1] is the way we usually evaluate an individual's wealth. But money is simply a place-holder for human endeavour. A pile of bank notes will do nothing until it is exchanged for something useful. It is just a storage medium, an exchangeable token deriving its universal value from the human intellect and the real physical labour that created it. And so I come back to the admirable Mr Jobs and Mr Gates. Both engaged with their specific inherited talents, and with that necessary sprinkling of serendipity, created a significant and positive change in the world. But Bill Gates took his accumulation of *storage medium* to the next level. Having used our unique talents to create something powerful, we then need to use that force to move society towards a better place.

The Bill and Melinda Gates Foundation is the vehicle with which Bill Gates brings his worth as a human being to fruition. He and his wife dedicate their working lives to supporting charitable causes around the world. Gates spent the first part of his life building wealth and influence and then began the process of turning that potential into something that significantly enriches his species on this precariously balanced planet. And that is what makes him so special. Some of you may disagree with me about Bill Gates. However, my point is about what we do with wealth and influence rather than praising Mr Gates in particular.

I have spent my life looking for my unique talent. I have done many things, and everything I do seems to show that I am a creative thinker and communicator. So far, I have not managed to build a powerful pile of wealth and/or influence, but I am still pursuing, with vigour, my impassioned quest to use my particular talents to inform, enlighten and entertain as many people as I can with my books.

So, the question you must all ask yourselves is, what are your special gifts? Believe me, you have them, we all do.

In a rare interview with Woody Allen he told a reporter that he was tired and would give up making films tomorrow if he could. He was asked why he continued to be such a prolific film maker, then? His answer was simple. "Because I'm good at it." It is his particular *talent* and it would be criminal if he squandered it.

The universe's gift to us is that against all odds, we made it. Now it is our turn to pay it back to the universe by using our unique talents. Hoarding them would be like owning a massive fresh water lake, yet dying of thirst, but before dying living long enough to witness the whole world dehydrate and turn to dust.

1. In reality I am referring to currency. Money has intrinsic value like gold or silver and therefore is more than just a token placeholder.

How to check if you are a good person?
May 2020

This is a question as old as human society. Some believe that there is no such thing as altruism, that every kind act is motivated by the chance of personal gain. Even if you perform a beneficial act with no payoff to yourself except the good feeling that you have done something selfless, it could still be argued that that 'good feeling' is the payoff. So, if simply experiencing self acknowledgement taints altruism, it would seem that it is indeed impossible to be truly selfless. But does that stop us from being good people? Doesn't a good act remain a good act even if the giver benefits?

I have thought about this a lot. A few years ago I became very confused about a very close relative of mine. Although I could recall many 'generous' acts from her I nevertheless had a feeling that she was not generous at all. On analysis it seemed that her motivation was always about how she felt at the time and that looked like selfishness. Then it finally dawned on me that she only gave when it was convenient for her, when it was easy and cost her nothing. True generosity is giving when giving is *needed*, not only when it is *convenient*.

I am reminded of the story of two old friends taking a walk and talking of friendship. One says to the other,

"We're good friends, right?"

"Yes! We are the best of friends," says the second man. "Why would you even ask such a thing?"

"Well, I was just thinking, if you had two houses, would you give me one?"

"Of course," the other answers. "What would I do with two houses. Of course I would give you one. You're my best friend."

"And what if you had two cars?" asks the first friend.

The second man looks at him and places a kindly hand on the other's shoulder.

"You are silly," he says, "You are the most important person in my life. Of course I'd give you a car if I had two."

They walk a little further in silence, then the first man speaks again.

"And what about if you had two bicycles—"

The second man cuts him off with a hard stare.

"Hang on! You know I've got two bicycles!"

It seems to me that the most important measure of being a good person is not what you do, but when you do it; giving (including 'of yourself') when someone has a greater need regardless of the cost to yourself, is the nearest we can get to altruism.

Far too often I find myself calculating my acts of kindness; weighing up the pros and cons, thinking about the worthiness of the person in need. I think I totally miss the simple truth; do I want to do this act of kindness or not. Being a good person is not about the quality or needs of the other person, it is about you. Sometimes you may decide not to help for many possible reasons, we are not saints and we are also finite. We may want to help, but not be in a position to do so. The important thing is what sort of person do we want to be. I once wrote, "I have no time for people who have no time for people."Although that is a humorous irony, it still holds true that the people that I warm to the most are those that always have time for others whenever they can.

In this current climate of the *coronavirus* and lockdowns it is all too easy to let the stress of the situation get to us and allow ourselves to become judgemental and self-preserving. Yet, this is a time when we would all benefit immensely from giving when giving is needed.

What gets you out of bed in the morning?
May 2020

In a recent newsletter I talked about altruism, and if it is really possible. Basically, I was musing about selfless giving, charity, and if it was a good thing or even possible considering that most actions bestow some benefit on the giver as well as the receiver and is therefore not selfless.

Today, I want to look at something even more fundamental, how to value yourself, or what gets you out of bed in the morning?

The serious business of living

Most, if not all, life on our planet survives hand to mouth. Every one of their actions are motivated by immediate need. 'I am hungry - I look for food and eat. I am thirsty - I seek out clean water and drink. I am tired - I find a safe place to rest.' For most living things, all of these activities take up the entirety of their lives. Once enough has been eaten, drunk and slept, the urge dissipates and the creature moves on to the next imperative on the survival to-do list. The mechanism that stops over indulgence is lack of opportunity. Most animals spend all of their time seeking out enough food and shelter to sustain life and do not have the chance to do anything to excess. That is all except one very notable exception, us, homo sapiens.

Blessed with excess!

We are the denizens of life economics. Billions of us have developed astonishing talents to create more food than we need, shelters far more elaborate than necessary for mere survival and sophisticated sprung mattresses on which to safely close our eyes every night, sometimes more as a routine than out of exhaustion. The self-regulating loop of visceral motivation verses scarcity of resources that has kept life on Earth within healthy bounds for millennia, has been torn apart by our large brains and opposable thumbs. Our brilliance at taming our environment and creating abundance has now far surpassed our basic needs, and so we find ourselves over consuming on epic levels as we have very little to stop us except our will. But will-power needs purpose to give it strength. Without purpose the human will is little more than wishful thinking which proves no match against millions of years of primitive animal desire. And so, we are driven by short-sighted hedonistic needs more than a far-sighted sense of self-worth. So, how do we combat the irresistible lure of excessive consumption? How do we achieve pre-emptive hindsight (making alterations to the present, while you are still there to change it)? How do we steer our universe-given ingenuity towards something of real lasting value rather than instant satisfaction?

I would suggest that each of us lies on a continuum from hedonism to productivity.

HEDONISM ———————— PRODUCTIVITY

At one extreme, hedonism would be all consuming like the mythical serpent eating itself. At the other end you would be all purpose and no point. Like everything in life, one needs balance. On a fundamental level, what drives most creatures are the feel-good sensations that we all crave. These *feelings* are the result of particular hormones being released by our bodies; namely dopamine, serotonin, oxytocin and endorphins. When we do something that causes the release of one or more of these chemicals we are rewarded with a great sensation of satisfaction and well-being, and that in turn leads us to do that particular action again and again. We are not attached to the action, but the feeling the *reward* hormones give us. Therefore, is it immaterial whether we are being hedonistic or productive as long as we get our *fix*? Are they the same? If you give in to an animal desire to binge on a box of chocolates you may well get a fantastic waterfall of feel-good chemicals coursing around your body, but when that passes you have a stomach ache, diabetes and may have added another inch to your waist. As well as those potentially adverse effects of your feast, you have created nothing productive or long-lasting. However, if you can push yourself to make that phone call you have been avoiding or tidy that heap of clothes in your wardrobe or go through that teetering mountain of receipts on your desk, you will have that same chemical rush on completion *plus* a really productive task done & dusted.

Why do I feel so tired?

I think we can take this even further. Sometimes the same activities can be either hedonistic or productive, and you get to choose. Take sleeping; you can go to bed because you are tired and need rest (productive) or because you are avoiding something and find being between warm sheets comforting (hedonistic). If you do the latter, you get a *rush* from the warm bed-hug, but you still have the thing you were avoiding hanging over you and now a possible feeling of guilt added in for good measure. But, go to bed because you need rest and get up at a reasonable hour when you have had a refreshing sleep, and it is a completely different ball game. In other words, go to bed as an act of productivity rather than as a giving in to hedonism. See sleeping as a restorative process that sets you up for the next day rather than a pleasure indulgence. If you find it hard to get up in the morning, it may be that you have let your mind view the bed as a hedonistic treat. You receive your hormone reward just the same, but in the morning you want to stay in bed to try and prolong the hormonal feel-good sensation. Conversely, if you see sleep as a productive restorative pursuit, you will wake rested and get a hormone rush from having looked after yourself.

Do not get me wrong. I am not suggesting that the above is easy. Getting up may still be difficult, but it will be because the new day is challenging rather than the bed not letting you go.

If you liked **Stupidly Deep Thinking**, please take a minute to leave a review on Amazon. It means so much to me to hear that readers enjoyed my books. Also, more reviews helps immensely with my visibility on Amazon, so other readers might find **Stupidly Deep Thinking**. Please take a moment, and let me know what you think.

Join the Readers' List for news & offers on my other books
http://eepurl.com/bMZF4z

Take a look at my other books on Amazon
http://viewauthor.at/Paul-Casselle-Books

Bedfellows Thriller Series

If The Bed Falls In

A psychological thriller that shines a spotlight on the shady dealings that may be the true reason so much is going wrong in our society.

Available from Amazon

Guerrillas by Night

A companion novella to the Bedfellows series. It tells the story of Book One from a fascinating new perspective. It follows the backstory of a very enigmatic female character from the pages of *If The Bed Falls In*.

Available from Amazon

As Mad as Hell

This second book in the series, takes us so much deeper as we follow a rogue MI6 agent using every resource he can to hunt down the culprits behind the *New World Order*. But he is a man battling with his own internal demons as well as the One Percenters.

Available from Amazon

Other books by Paul Casselle

Conversations with Eric

Full of mystery, painfully funny situations and twisting plots,
Simon picks his way through an ever thickening soup of intrigue
and murder. At every turn, he tries to get out, but he continues to
be sucked in by murderous villains and the psychologically
damaged criminal class.

Available from Amazon

Everyone Else's Everyone Else (Short Story)

From morning to sundown, the machinations of London's
humanity ebb and flow, intermingling with each other in the way
only we happily, insane humans can.

We all have our stories, but to a stranger on the street...who are
we, and who are they?

Available from Amazon

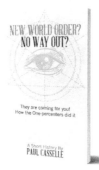

New World Order? No Way Out? (Non-Fiction)

Many of us are becoming aware of a growing global problem
with national economies and terrorism, but some believe we are
being led down this path by powerful people determined to
destroy our free society in favour of their own greed. So, is this
conspiracy nonsense?

Available from Amazon

Blue Skies over Dark Days (An unreliable memoir)

These are true tales - well, mostly. In this first volume of
autobiographical episodes, I have allowed a little artistic licence to
hopefully turn some extraordinary events from my life into funny
and often moving pieces.

Available from Amazon

The Unforgiving Minute (A Sci-Fi Thriller)

Professor Edward Vivian Phillips, head of Physics at Trinity College, Cambridge has just invented the unthinkable! But celebrations are cut short when he is arrested for the murder of his research fellow, Alan Newton.

Phillips claims he didn't do it. That he couldn't have done it.

Professor Phillips was using his new invention at the time of Newton's murder. However, his claim means that he is either innocent or a madman!

Available from Amazon

Printed in Great Britain
by Amazon

28263701R00088